The Armor of God

Winning the Spiritual Battle

Dr. David Chapman

**The Armor of God:
Winning the Spiritual Battle**

Dr. David Chapman

Printed in the United States of America. All rights reserved under International Copyright Law. Contents and/or cover may not be reproduced in whole or in part in any form without the expressed written consent of the Publisher.

All Bible quotations are from the New King James Version unless otherwise noted.

Copyright © 2020

**TRU Publishing
1726 S. 1st Ave.
Safford, Arizona 85546**

Table of Contents

Chapter One: Be Strong in the Lord 6

Chapter Two: The Belt of Truth 23

Chapter Three: Breastplate of Righteousness.............31

Chapter Four: Gospel Shoes..41

Chapter Five: Shield of Faith 56

Chapter Six: Helmet of Salvation................................69

Chapter Seven: Sword of the Spirit (Word of God).....90

Chapter Eight: Prayer 105

Introduction

At the time of this writing, the world is going through the COVID-19 pandemic. It has taken a very heavy toll on many levels – individual health, world economies, and among other things, the condition of the church. Effectively, church has not been allowed to function, as we have known it for decades. Yet I am convinced that God never permits anything upon the earth that will ultimately hinder His church. Jesus said, "Upon this rock I will build my church; and the gates of hell shall not prevail against it" (Matthew 16:18).

During this, and all other times, every believer needs to hear the alarm of the Spirit. We are called to battle. We must each dress ourselves in the full armor of God in order to withstand in the evil day. This book will provide you with practical application of how to demonstrate the victory that Christ has already won through His death and resurrection.

We are more than conquerors through Christ, but we must practically apply the truth of God in order to live victoriously. Join me in this study of the full armor of God.

Chapter One: Be Strong in the Lord

When I was first saved I had a glorious encounter with God. I was very depressed and suicidal for a long time leading up to my salvation. On that particular night I was getting high at a friend's house and in my mind contemplating how I was going to end my life, at the age of 20. I had two black eyes and stitches between my eyes and in my lip from fighting three nights earlier. At around 2:00am the Lord appeared before me. I was awestruck and immediately left that house. I was on foot, so I walked in the stormy May wind for several blocks asked the Lord to forgive me and come into my heart. At a certain climactic point I fell to my knees as the Holy Spirit entered me and the weight of sin was lifted off of me. I was free.

For the next ten days I was on cloud nine. It was the first time in my life that I'd felt any peace or happiness. I didn't know any other Christians yet so I was consuming everything I could from the Bible and

Christian television. It all seemed to good to be true. On the eleventh day I was sitting on my bed reading the Bible when out of nowhere, a fierce attack came against my mind. Horrible blasphemies and evil thoughts pierced my mind like flaming arrows. Where was this coming from, I questioned? Did I bring this on with something I'd done? I was shaken and devastated.

This encounter with Satan began a series of similar attacks that carried on for days. I reached out to a nearby pastor for help. He told me that it was all in my mind. I cried out to God for deliverance. I was battled day after day. It felt too much for me. I had nowhere to turn for help. One night it began again and I called a prayer hotline. After explaining what was happening, this prayer counselor began to pray in the authority of Jesus' name. As she prayed, I could feel what felt like liquid fire pouring into my body and setting me on fire. It was the Holy Spirit setting me free. For several days after that, every time Satan would try to attack me, this same fire would fill me and protect me. Satan never attacked me in that same way again.

> **The victory has already been won.**

I learned very early in my walk with Christ that spiritual warfare was real. I also learned that as believers, we have authority in Christ. The victory has already been won. We simply must enforce it through the name of Jesus and by keeping on the whole armor of God.

The Armor of God

Paul, in his letter to the Ephesians, outlined the Christian soldier's responsibilities and armor.

> **Ephesians 6:10-11**
> **10 Finally, my brethren, be strong in the Lord and in the power of His might.**
> **11 Put on the whole armor of God, that you may be able to stand against the wiles of the devil.**

Paul uses a word in these statements on two occasions that comes from the original Greek root word *dunamis*. It is the word from which "dynamite" is derived. Paul is speaking of an explosive power in the believer's life. The word is translated "strong" in verse 10 and "able" in verse 11. This power comes from one source – the Holy Spirit.

It requires the power of the Holy Spirit to overcome the wiles of the devil. I continually emphasize how the devil gains the advantage over the believer – it is through schemes, deceit, lies, and trickery. He has to use these methods, because he has been stripped of all legitimate authority.

When Paul wrote, "Put on the whole armor of God," he was staring at a Roman soldier while in prison. In Ephesians 6:20, Paul referred to himself as, "An ambassador in chains." The Roman army was the greatest military force in the world for 500 years. As Paul examined the armor of the soldiers, the Holy Spirit began to speak to him about the Christian's armor.

> **The Roman army was the greatest military force in the world for 500 years.**

Not only was the armor of the Roman soldier the most advanced in the world at that time, but the soldiers were extensively trained and conditioned. He had to endure six months of vigorous training after enlistment. His conditioning was so thorough that he had to march 24 miles in five hours, dressed in full armor and carrying 60 pounds of supplies on his back.

In the early days of the Roman army, only landowners could be soldiers. They figured that the landowners would fight harder in order to protect their property. Eventually, enlistment was opened up and became a paid profession. But a man had to enlist for 25 years in order to become a Roman soldier. He was also not allowed to marry. Total dedication and complete focus was required to be part of the Roman army. This reminds me of the verse in 2 Timothy:

> **2 Timothy 2:4 (ESV) No soldier gets entangled in civilian pursuits, since his aim is to please the one who enlisted him.**

The Roman army was very organized. They were divided into legions, which were 5,000 in number. They were further divided into centuries of 100, with a Centurion placed in charge. Individualism was not permitted. They all worked and fought for a common cause. In fact, the armor itself was so complicated that a soldier had to have help in order to get it all fastened.

This serves as a reminder to believers that this battle is not intended to be fought alone. We cannot be fully dressed in the armor of God and fight in this battle without the help of our brothers and sisters in Christ.

> **This battle is not intended to be fought alone.**

Standing

Notice that Paul said that we are to put on the whole armor of God in order that we might *stand* against the wiles of the devil. He didn't say that we might *advance*. The Christian life is not always set in advance mode. There are times when we are supposed to stand – stand our ground.

There are two modes for the believer:

1. Advancing
2. Standing

There is no mode for *retreating*. The armor of God protects us in order that we don't have to retreat. If the believer is in retreat mode, surely he has fallen prey to the devices of the devil.

There may be times when you *feel* like you are retreating, but in actuality, you are standing. It's just that you've become weary in the battle. But God will not allow you to be tested with more than you are able to overcome (1 Corinthians 10:13).

> **There is no mode for *retreating*.**

Don't be caught in a situation where you think you are standing, but in reality you are on faulty ground. An example of faulty ground would be to believe that a religious tradition is the same foundation as God's Word.

> **1 Corinthians 10:12 Therefore let him who thinks he stands take heed lest he fall.**

There are some 21 times in the New Testament epistles that the word stand is used in such a way to descript the Christian's spiritual position.

Spiritual Wrestling

Paul next goes on to describe the nature of our conflict:

> **Ephesians 6:12 For we do not wrestle with flesh and blood, but against principalities, against powers, against the rulers of the darkness of this age, against spiritual hosts of wickedness in the heavenly places.**

Paul could have used any of a number of terms here instead of *wrestling*. He had perfect command of the Greek language and could have picked a word such as *fight*, *contend* or *oppose*. Why did Paul choose *wrestle*? Quite simply, it denotes actual contact combat.

> **Our conflict with demons is on a contact basis.**

One can, fight without contact; one can contend or oppose without contact, but have you ever seen anyone try to wrestle without contact? It is impossible! Our conflict with demons is on a contact basis. They are always coming against us in a tangible way, buffeting us in the flesh.

2 Corinthians 12:7 And lest I should be exalted above measure by the abundance of the revelations, a thorn in the flesh was given to me, a messenger of Satan to buffet me, lest I be exalted above measure.

It is interesting that the Greek word for "buffet" here is *kolaphizó* and means, "To strike with the fist." Again, Paul gives us such graphic word pictures. Here, the messenger [Gr. *angelos*] or angel of Satan is seen as physically punching Paul with his fist. How can anyone fail to see the nature of the conflict that we, as believers, are in?

This wrestling match that Paul spoke of was an effective allegory because the readers of his letter understood how a Greek wrestling match was conducted. A winner was declared when one of the wrestlers successfully pinned the neck area of his opponent. The loser was made to endure a terrible and painful blinding by the gouging out of the eyes. All that lose this spiritual wrestling match also endure a blinding, a loss of spiritual discernment.

> The loser was made to endure a terrible and painful blinding by the gouging out of the eyes.

Other Instances of Wrestling in the Bible

In Genesis, Jacob wrestled with the pre-incarnate Christ. Jacob, as his name literally means, was a deceiver. He'd always manipulated his way to get the birthright from his brother and the blessing from his father. But ultimately it caught up with him and he wrestled the Lord all night.

> **Genesis 32:24 Then Jacob was left alone; and a Man wrestled with him until the breaking of day.**

Have you ever wrestled the Lord? Maybe it was a difficult decision, or a matter of consecration to God's will. At the end, Jacob was brought into submission and had his name changed to Israel, meaning, "One who prevails with God or prince with God." From a physical standpoint, the way Jacob was brought into submission was the wounding of his hip joint. He had a limp for the rest of his life, but he learned to trust in the Lord and not his own strength.

> **Hebrews 11:21 By faith Jacob, when he was dying, blessed each of the sons of Joseph, and worshiped, leaning on the top of his staff.**

The other reference to wrestling that I want to mention is found in the New Testament. Paul mentions Epaphras wrestling in prayer for the believers at Colossae.

> **Colossians 4:12 (NIV) Epaphras, who is one of you and a servant of Christ Jesus, sends greetings. He is always wrestling in prayer for you, that you may stand firm in all the will of God, mature and fully assured.**

I bring up these two references in order to show that spiritual wrestling is a biblical reality. Whether one is wrestling with God, wrestling in prayer or wrestling with the devil, it requires spiritual intensity.

The Devil's Org Chart

Revealed in Ephesians 6:12 are four levels of demon power:

> **Ephesians 6:12 For we do not wrestle against flesh and blood, but against principalities, against powers, against the rulers of the darkness of this age, against spiritual hosts of wickedness in the heavenly places.**

Let's look at each level starting with the highest rank.

1. **Principalities**: These are the highest rank of demons. This word comes from the Greek word *archē*, which means, "Beginning or first." Principalities rule over entire nations, such as

the *Prince of Persia* in Daniel's day (Daniel 10:20). Their job is to mastermind and to see that evil covers the earth and prevails against the church (a losing cause, by the way).

2. **Powers**: Second in command are *powers*. This word comes from the Greek word *exousia*, which means, "Authority, conferred power, designated jurisdiction." These demonic beings carry out the mission of Satan under the direction of Principalities.

3. **Rulers of Darkness**: Demons that rule in the area of a particular stronghold, such as gambling, pornography or false religion. These demons are subject matter experts in their respective areas of destruction. These spirits have lower level demons under their command. The Greek word being translated here is *kosmokrátōr*, which is a compound word. *Kosmos* means "world" and *kratéō* means "to put under control." These demons influence the lives of worldly people.

4. **Wicked Spirits in Heavenly Places**: These are lower level demons that we most commonly deal with on a personal, daily level. "Heavenly places" refers to the atmosphere above (see Ephesians 2:2). Wicked means, "Iniquity; painful trouble." The job of wicked spirits is to afflict and oppress people. Sin or iniquity is the

tool these demons use to destroy people's lives.

Org Chart

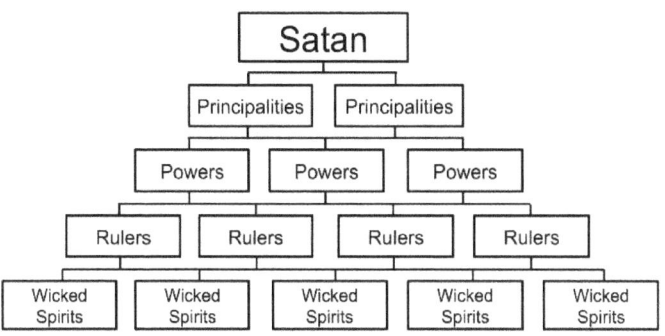

Listen to the words of Gabriel, the Arch Angel in charge of Communication, when addressing Daniel regarding his prayer and the spiritual battle that played out in the spirit realm:

> **Daniel 10:12-14**
> **12 Then he said to me, "Do not fear, Daniel, for from the first day that you set your heart to understand, and to humble yourself before your God, your words were heard; and I have come because of your words.**
> **13 But the prince of the kingdom of Persia withstood me twenty-one days; and behold, Michael, one of the chief princes, came to help**

> me, for I had been left alone there with the kings of Persia.
> **14** Now I have come to make you understand what will happen to your people in the latter days, for the vision refers to many days yet to come."

Satan did not want this revelation concerning the end times to get to Daniel and opposed the messenger of God, Gabriel. Assistance had to be obtained from Michael, the Arch Angel in charge of Warfare, to break through. It is important to remember that there will be no significant breakthrough from God in your life that will not be contested by the enemy. But let it be clear that God heard Daniel on the first day and sent the answer. It is upon us to stand and not to give place to the devil with double-mindedness and unbelief.

> **It is upon us to stand and not to give place to the devil with double-mindedness and unbelief.**

The good news is that, as believers, we are fighting from *the place* of victory and not to get *to* the victory. What do you do from the place of victory? You stand.

Standing

> **Ephesians 6:13-14**

**13 Therefore take up the whole armor of God, that you may be able to withstand in the evil day, and having done all, to stand.
14 Stand therefore…**

In order to stand for the breakthrough, one must have "done all" before taking the final stand. Have you done what the Word says to do? This means being a doer of the Word – especially in the area of your struggle. Let's use a financial problem as an example. If you need a financial breakthrough, you can say, "I'm standing in faith for a financial miracle," but if you aren't a giver and a good steward, you have no ground upon which to stand. Ultimately, it's a form of self-deception.

> **James 1:22 But be doers of the word, and not hearers only, deceiving yourselves.**

Put on the Whole Armor

In answer to this hierarchy of demonic power arrayed against us, the believers are to put on the whole armor of God as detailed in Ephesians 6:14-18:

> **Ephesians 6:14-19
> 14 Stand therefore, having girded your waist with truth, having put on the breastplate of righteousness,**

15 and having shod your feet with the preparation of the gospel of peace;

16 above all, taking the shield of faith with which you will be able to quench all the fiery darts of the wicked one.

17 And take the helmet of salvation, and the sword of the Spirit, which is the word of God;

18 praying always with all prayer and supplication in the Spirit, being watchful to this end with all perseverance and supplication for all the saints.

19 and for me, that utterance may be given to me, that I may open my mouth boldly to make known the mystery of the gospel

A couple of years ago I had an encounter with a demon during the middle of the night. At first I thought it might have been a dream, but I realized it wasn't. A large demon, which appeared to me as a very dark figure, jumped on my back while I was in bed. My wife had already gotten up and was doing her morning workout. This demon made a fist and put it in the middle of my chest and put his other hand on top of it and began to squeeze. I was going to have a heart attack. I couldn't breath and for a second, I felt hopeless.

But in the middle of this attack, I felt an authority rise up within my spirit. I shouted, "In the name of Jesus, I command you to go!" Instantly, the pressure on my chest was gone and I was overcome with God's peace. I went back to sleep for a little while. When I got up, I was going to tell my wife what happened. But instead she told me. She had come back from the gym about the same time as this was happening and heard my shout the name of Jesus. She said there had been a heavy oppression in the room but after I used the name of Jesus, the whole room was filled with peace.

How many times do we allow Satan to afflict us instead of using our authority in Christ? We must learn to put on the full armor of God in order to live victoriously.

Chapter One Review

1. What does the Greek word *dunamis* mean?

_____

_____

2. Name one requirement to be a Roman soldier.

_____

_____

3. What are the two acceptable modes for every believer?

_____

_____

4. Why did Paul use the word wrestling when describing spiritual warfare?

_____

_____

_____

_____

5. List the four levels of demonic power.

_____

_____

_____

_____

Chapter Two: The Belt of Truth

Ephesians 6:14 Stand therefore, having girded your waist with truth...

Some other translations:

> *Stand firm then, with the belt of truth buckled around your waist*

(New International Version).

Stand therefore, having fastened on the belt of truth (English Standard Version).

Stand therefore, having the utility belt of truth buckled around your waist (New Heart English Bible).

The belt is probably the last thing you think of when you think about the mighty Roman soldier's armor. Yet Paul lists the belt first. The belt is what held everything in place. If a soldier lost his belt, his breastplate would not be secure. There would also be no place to secure his sword. Truth and integrity are like that. When they're absent, everything is exposed. You won't get far in God's army without the belt of truth.

> **The belt is what held everything in place.**

Truth and truthfulness are inseparable. You cannot claim to know the truth of God's Word while at the same time live an untruthful life. Integrity means that you keep saying and doing the same things – the right things in the worst of times, just like in the best of times.

I've known lots of very gifted preachers who eventually lost their ministries because they lacked the belt of truth. If you are doing God's work and you can't do it with integrity, at some point you're going to get caught with your pants down.

What did the Roman soldier's belt look like? It was large with many loops to hold weapons. The Lord has many weapons available for the Spirit-filled believer. It's amazing that some Christians continue to rely on their natural abilities to fight spiritual battles. Paul wrote, *"For the weapons of our warfare are not carnal [natural] but mighty in God for pulling down strongholds"* (2 Corinthians 10:4).

> **The Lord has many weapons available for the Spirit-filled believer.**

Below are some of the primary weapons that every believer possesses.

- The Word
- The name of Jesus
- The blood of Jesus
- The gifts of the Spirit
- Prayer

The believer's belt is made with the truth of God's Word – all of God's Word. 2 Timothy 3:16 says, *"All Scripture is given by inspiration of God, and is profitable for doctrine, for reproof, for correction, for instruction in righteousness."* I especially like the way that the Good News Translation renders this verse:

2 Timothy 3:16 (Good News Translation) All Scripture is inspired by God and is useful for teaching the truth, rebuking error, correcting faults, and giving instruction for right living.

The belt of truth is useful for:

1. Teaching the truth
2. Rebuking error
3. Correcting faults
4. Giving instruction for right living

An error is an unintentional mistake, while a fault is a shortcoming or flaw. The belt of God's truth will warn us of those mistakes we unintentionally make, before we make them. Oh how I wish I'd been wearing the belt God's truth all my life. I could have been spared from the consequences of so many bad decisions. With regards to faults, the Greek word translated "correct" (*epanorthósis*) means, "To restore to its (original) proper condition." The truth has the ability to restore broken people. People are often told their whole life that they have to be a certain way because of genetics or nurture. This simply isn't true. The Bible says that if anyone is in Christ, that person is

> **The truth has the ability to restore broken people.**

a new creation; old things pass away and all things become new (2 Corinthians 5:17).

Ultimately, the belt of truth is useful to help us with right living. Belts are helpful when active. No belt is needed when one is inactive. There's a reason that there's no belt loops on your pajamas. We must be doers of the Word of God and not hearers only (James 1:22).

There are two Greek words in the New Testament that are translated "Word" in relation to the *Word of God*.

1. **Logos:** this word means the *written* word of God. It is the entirety of the Scripture. Every word is inspired by God (2 Timothy 3:16). *Logos* is found 330 times in the New Testament.

2. **Rhema:** this word means the *spoken* word of God. It is personal and revealed by the Spirit. The spoken word is always in harmony with and subservient to the written word. *Rhema* is found 70 times in the New Testament.

The belt of truth is primarily the *logos* – the written Word of God. The sword of the Spirit is the *rhema* of God. The rhema of God comes on an as-needed basis. The Lord is always faithful to speak a word in season to us just when we need it. The logos of God is always available and should be studied to make one wise and give instruction for living. This is the belt that must always be worn.

The Roman soldier's belt was tied in several places to keep it secure. This is a reminder that all of God's truth must be appropriated. In the last days, Paul warned that in the last days there would be a great falling away. Churchgoers will want their ears tickled with their favorites doctrines (2 Timothy 4:3). God has never called anyone to be an ear scratcher. Don't be a people pleaser!

> **The belt of truth is primarily the *logos* – the written Word of God.**

Further, there were markings to designate past campaigns (we are overcomers). In each of the seven letters Jesus wrote to the churches of Asia Minor (Revelation 2-3), He mentioned what it meant to be an overcomer. The reality is that to be an overcomer, you must *come over* something. I'm writing this material in the spring of 2020, right in the middle of the worst pandemic to ever hit the world with the Coronavirus. People are panicking, but the true believers have a peace because they know that God is in control. We have some markings on our belt to remind us that the same God who has delivered us in the past will deliver us yet again!

Truth and integrity of heart is what holds the armor together. In these last days, there is a lot of twisting of the truth of God's Word. Satan uses his emissaries to deceive the hearts and minds of people, lest they believe the truth of God's Word and be delivered. When one departs from God's truth and personal integrity all else is out of place.

> **Truth and integrity of heart is what holds the armor together.**

Regardless of how eloquent or dynamic a preacher is, if he lacks the belt of truth, do not follow him.

Jesus said that it was the Truth that we know that would make us free.

> **John 8:31-32**
> **31 Then Jesus said to those Jews who believed Him, "If you abide in My word, you are My disciples indeed.**
> **32 And you shall know the truth, and the truth shall make you free."**

This isn't truth that we just intellectually know. It is the truth of God that becomes revelation knowledge, renews the mind and and is put into practice. Later in this book, we will discuss the arena of the mind. The Believer's armor must be held together by revelation truth from God's Word.

Chapter Two Review

1. What piece of the armor holds everything in place?

_____

_____

2. Name at least three weapons given to every believer.

_____

_____

_____

3. What is a rhema word from God?

_____

_____

4. What did markings on the belt represent and why is that important?

_____

_____

_____

_____

Chapter Three: Breastplate of Righteousness

Ephesians 6:14 Stand therefore... having put on the breastplate of righteousness

The words *righteous* (262 times) and *righteousness* (315 times) appear in the New King James Version a total of 577 times.

On its most basic level, righteousness means, "Right standing with God and right living for God."

Right Standing *with* God
Right Living *for* God

Right standing with God can only happen one way: through the shed blood of Jesus on the cross. Good works cannot put anyone into right standing with God. It is purely by the grace of God that we can be saved. It is not 75% God's grace and 25% my works. It is not even 99% grace and 1% my works. Right standing with God comes by God's grace – 100%.

Right living for God happens as a result of being placed into right standing with God. Whenever we try to flip the order of that sequence it places us back under the law – separated from God. I want to live for God because I have a relationship with the Father through Jesus Christ. Right living becomes an overflow of right standing. This is true righteousness.

> **Righteousness is still needed to enter the ark of salvation.**

Let's back up and look at the very beginning of the topic of righteousness.

There is a rule of interpretation used on the study of the Bible; it's called the Law of First Mention. This means that the first time a word is used, it carries more weight in forming the definition. The first time the word *righteous* was used was in Genesis 7:1 in relation to Noah.

> **Genesis 7:1 Then the LORD said to Noah, "Come into the ark, you and all your household, because I have seen that you are righteous before Me in this generation.**

Noah and his family entering the ark and being saved from the flood is a type of salvation. From this verse we see that salvation can only be attained through righteousness. The standard for salvation has not been lowered. Righteousness is still needed to enter God's ark of salvation. The question becomes, how then do we attain this righteousness?

> **It is impossible to walk in righteousness without being girded with the truth.**

The first instance of the word righteousness is also found in Genesis, in relation to a man named Abraham.

> **Genesis 15:6 And he believed in the LORD, and He accounted it to him for righteousness.**

So we see here in the life of Abraham that he was accounted righteous by faith. The word for *accounted* means "to impute." It is an accounting term. He did not arrive at his right standing with God through his works, but instead through faith. Galatians 3:29 says that we are the seed of Abraham through faith.

The breastplate was connected to the belt. It is impossible to walk in righteousness without being girded with the truth. The two are inseparable. Deceitfulness in any form will cause chinks in the breastplate of righteousness. Whenever a believer starts distorting the truth, the guard over the heart gets lowered and Satan gains an advantage. It has to start with being honest with yourself. Self-deceit will produce a self-righteousness that makes a person feel right with God but is based in pride instead. The Pharisees operated in this type of false righteousness.

The Roman soldier's breastplate was not clunky but lightweight enough to allow freedom of movement. He needed to be agile and mobile. Other armies would weigh down their soldiers with heavy armor and inhibit their mobility. This gave the Roman soldier a supreme advantage. Conversely, the righteousness of God doesn't weigh us down. Legalistic religion is like the army that suits its soldiers in heavy and clunky armor that's impossible to bear and hard to use. Not only is that armor almost impossible to bear, but also you never win the battle. There will always be some rule that you didn't keep.

The Pharisees had 613 laws from the Torah and thousands of traditions that they had made up. Talk about being weighed down! However, the Bible says in 1 John 5:3 that *God's commandments are not burdensome*. The Greek word for *burdensome* means "to be heavy or weighty." The person trying to attain righteousness by the law is so depleted from the weight of the armor that he has no energy left to fight the battle. The Pharisees actually started off devoutly and making a positive difference in religion and education a couple hundred years before Jesus. But over time, pride took root and resulted in corruption by the time Jesus was on the earth. Guard your heart that you don't allow relationship to turn into rules and traditions of men.

> **God's commandments are not burdensome.**

The breastplate covers the vital organs such as the heart. Implicit throughout the Bible is the instruction to guard your heart. Proverbs explicitly says the following:

> **Don't allow relationship to turn into rules.**

Proverbs 4:23 (NIV) Above all else, guard your heart, for everything you do flows from it.

Guarding our hearts means watching out for what we expose it to. There is a lot of subtlety in how the devil operates when trying to infiltrate the human heart (Genesis 3). The enemy tries to engage the faculties of our rationalization. Compromise seems benign in the beginning, but it can cost you dearly in the end. As Solomon wrote: "The little foxes spoil the vines" (Song of Solomon 2:15).

It is the righteousness of God in Christ that covers us. All of our righteousness is as filthy rags (Isaiah 64:6). There is absolutely nothing we can do through the power of self to put us into right standing with God. Righteousness in the court of heaven could only be attained by one man. Moreover, for that righteousness to be imputed to others, that one man had to bear their sins on the cross.

> **There is absolutely nothing we can do through the power of self to put us into right standing with God.**

> **2 Corinthians 5:21 For He made Him who knew no sin to be sin for us, that we might become the righteousness of God in Him.**

On the cross, Jesus was treated like a sinner, though perfect and righteous. And *through* the cross, we are treated as righteous by God, though we are sinful and broken when we come to Him.

Of course, the righteousness of God that is imputed through the blood of Jesus must be appropriated and applied. His righteousness must be go beyond a legal fact to an experiential reality in our lives if true protection is to be found through the breastplate. But it's always a matter of resting in the righteousness of God in Christ that allows us to live out the fruit of righteousness.

Satan attacks the Believer's right standing with God probably more than any other area. He tries to place a blanket of guilt upon us to get us to draw back from God. Condemnation is one of the enemy's greatest weapons against the breastplate of righteousness. Satan will try to remind you of your past in order to take your eyes off of Jesus. If you were in heaven's courtroom, Satan would be the prosecutor trying to convict you of your past wrongdoing. Jesus is your defense attorney or advocate. We need look no further than John's writings to validate this scenario.

Satan – the Accuser

> **Revelation 12:10 Then I heard a loud voice saying in heaven, "Now salvation, and strength, and the kingdom of our God, and the power of His Christ have come, for the accuser**

of our brethren, who accused them before our God day and night, has been cast down.

Jesus – our Advocate

1 John 2:1 My little children, these things I write to you, so that you may not sin. And if anyone sins, we have an Advocate with the Father, Jesus Christ the righteous.

When Satan accuses the child of God, Jesus our advocate points to the bloodstained mercy seat in heaven. The ransom price has been paid in full. Jesus Christ the righteous has placed us into right standing with the Father. Heaven's Judge has declared us innocent of all charges.

> It is God's perfect will that you don't sin.

As John wrote, "These things I write to you, so that you may not sin." It is God's perfect will that you don't sin. But He knows that perfection is not within our reach in this life. Thus our advocate never leaves our side. Religion and the church world may abandon us when we sin. But Jesus will never leave you nor forsake you (Hebrews 13:5).

Righteousness produces boldness!

Proverbs 28:1 The wicked flee when no one pursues, But the righteous are bold as a lion.

In this spiritual battle we are informed that "the devil walks about **like** a roaring lion, seeking whom he **may** devour" (1 Peter 5:8). While the devil is like a roaring lion and he may devour some, the Bible tells us that it's the righteous who are truly bold as a lion. Because of the breastplate of righteousness, the believer never needs to retreat.

> **Our advocate never leaves our side.**

Chapter Three Review

1. What are the two sides of righteousness?

_____

_____

_____

_____

2. It is impossible to walk in righteousness without being girded with the _____.

3. What area of a believer's life does Satan attack more than any other?

_____

_____

_____

Chapter Four: Gospel Shoes

Ephesians 6:15 and having shod your feet with the preparation of the gospel of peace.

As previously mentioned, the believer is called to do two things as it relates to the use of his shoes or foot armor:

1. Advancing
2. Standing

The Roman soldier was never to be in a mode of retreat. But that does not mean that he was always to be advancing. There were times in battle when the most needed and strategic thing to do was to stand his ground. Only a foolish soldier would move forward without discernment of the enemy's whereabouts. Without effective footwear both of these would be nearly impossible.

The Roman soldier's shoes were heavy-soled with metal studs on the bottom for good footing on uneven or slippery ground.

Roman Soldier's Sole

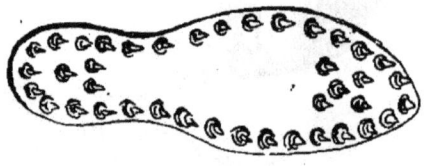

Spiritual warfare doesn't always come in the form that you expect. There are unexpected attacks that must be accounted for. We all have blind spots and we don't always know what's waiting around the corner. There must be preparedness for the uneven or slippery terrain of spiritual battles. Sometimes that comes in the form of standing. But we don't always have the level ground we hope for to do so. Satan's desire is to catch us off guard and knock us off our balance. A prepared soldier of the Lord will be ready for these attacks.

Soul-winning

The center of the believer's life must be focused on evangelism. This puts our attention and concerns on the needs of others. When our focus is self-centered in our Christian walk, there is a hole in the armor. The battle we are in is for a cause. The devil isn't just trying to ruin your day. There are bigger stakes. He wants to take souls to hell. There are lost people in your path every day.

> Satan's desire is to catch us off guard and knock us off our balance.

Proverbs 11:30 He who wins souls is wise.

Shoes reflect one's walk. The Believer's walk must be about more than individual needs. Get involved in the work of the ministry – put your gospel shoes to work! The Great Commission says to "Go therefore and make disciples of all the nations…" (Matthew 28:19). Shoes are for *going*. When I put my shoes on my wife asks me, "Where are you going?" When I put a certain type of shoe on, it gives a clue. If I put work boots on, I'm probably not going to the office. If I put sneakers on, I might be going to workout. When we put on our spiritual armor shoes, it should be known that we are going to fight for lost souls.

Having our shoes on speaks to readiness and preparedness. Are you willing to go where God is sending you? Some say they are willing to go across the world to China, but in reality they won't yet go across the street to share the gospel with their neighbor. Those around us who are lost cannot be saved unless they hear the gospel first. God puts you in strategic situations in order to share the good news.

> **Are you willing to go where God is sending you?**

> **Romans 10:14-15**
> **14 How then shall they call on Him in whom they have not believed? And how shall they believe in Him of whom they have not heard? And how shall they hear without a preacher?**
> **15 And how shall they preach unless they are sent? As it is written: "How beautiful are the feet of those who preach the gospel of peace, who bring glad tidings of good things!"**

Peace

It's interesting that Paul refers to the gospel as the "gospel of peace" here in this passage about spiritual warfare. The Christian soldier marches in the efforts of God's peace, but the enemy resists these efforts and thus, we have the warfare.

As I write this material in the year 2020, the world is far from peace. This has been a year of pandemics and riots in America. Some think change will happen as a result of government reform or protests, but true change will only happen through the power of the gospel of Jesus Christ. The absence of peace is a heart issue that cannot be fixed through the world's means.

The most well known hymn of all time is Amazing Grace, written in 1779. The composer of the hymn was John Newton. He was a blasphemous sailor who was a slave trader. One night at the helm, in a terrible storm, his mind raced back to the Bible verses his mother had taught him as a child. His mother had prayed that John would become of minister of the gospel. That night in 1748, John Newton surrendered his life to Jesus. Ultimately, John Newton became

> **The absence of peace is a heart issue that cannot be fixed through the world's means.**

instrumental in the abolition of slavery in Britain. The real change, however, began in his heart.

Amazing Grace, how sweet the sound
That saved a wretch like me
I once was lost, but now am found
Was blind but now I see

Was Grace that taught my heart to fear
And Grace, my fears relieved
How precious did that Grace appear
The hour I first believed

Through many dangers, toils and snares
We have already come
T'was Grace that brought us safe thus far
And Grace will lead us home
And Grace will lead us home

Amazing Grace, how sweet the sound
That saved a wretch like me
I once was lost but now am found
Was blind but now I see

Was blind, but now I see

The Early Church

How did the early church grow so fast? How did the early church even survive, given all the persecution? Satan thought he could stamp out the church through harsh and severe persecution and martyrdom. The Roman Empire was steeped in pagan religions and debauchery. Sometimes people act like sin was invented in the twentieth century. The Roman Empire was as corrupt as any culture in the last two thousand years.

So how did the church not only survive, but also exponentially multiply? The book of Acts is a great place to start in finding the answer to this question.

> **Acts 1:8 But you shall receive power when the Holy Spirit has come upon you; and you shall be witnesses to Me in Jerusalem, and in all Judea and Samaria, and to the end of the earth."**

> **Acts 2:4, 41, 46-47**
> **4 And they were all filled with the Holy Spirit and began to speak with other tongues, as the Spirit gave them utterance.**
> **41 Then those who gladly received his word were baptized; and that day about three thousand souls were added to them.**

46 So continuing daily with one accord in the temple, and breaking bread from house to house, they ate their food with gladness and simplicity of heart,

47 praising God and having favor with all the people. And the Lord added to the church daily those who were being saved.

Acts 3:6-8; 4:4

6 Then Peter said, "Silver and gold I do not have, but what I do have I give you: In the name of Jesus Christ of Nazareth, rise up and walk."

7 And he took him by the right hand and lifted him up, and immediately his feet and ankle bones received strength.

8 So he, leaping up, stood and walked and entered the temple with them—walking, leaping, and praising God. 9 And all the people saw him walking and praising God.

4 However, many of those who heard the word believed; and the number of the men came to be about five thousand.

Just within the first four chapters of Acts we see that the source of the power to witness was the Holy Spirit (1:8). When he came (2:4), power filled those in the upper room. Peter stood to preach under the anointing of the Spirit and three thousand souls were added to the church (2:41). But beyond the mass conversions, the church met daily in various forms (2:46) and the Lord added to the church daily those who were being saved (2:47).

Moreover, miracles were common among the early disciples. Peter and John were used to heal the lame man (3:6-8) and this lead to five thousand hearing the Word and being saved (4:4).

Keys for Early Church Evangelism
- The Baptism with the Holy Spirit
- Community and Relationship
- Healing Miracles

After such a powerful start, God wasn't done! He then gave Peter a vision and sent him to the gentiles (Acts 10). Those at Cornelius' house were saved and baptized with the Holy Spirit. But right before that, a well-known persecutor of the church, Saul of Tarsus was miraculously saved (Acts 9). All of this combined to move the church out into the entire known world.

Paul, along with his coworkers, sailed on three major mission trips and established churches throughout the gentile nations.

1. Acts 13 (Cyprus and southern Asia Minor)

2. Acts 16 (southern Asia Minor and Macedonia, primarily Corinth)
3. Acts 19 (Asia Minor and Macedonia again, primarily Ephesus).

Based on his letters, it's clear that Paul went on many other missionary journeys as well. The Roman Empire covered about 2.2 million square miles and 60 million people claimed Roman citizenship. Rome's 75,000-mile road network made spreading the gospel much easier. It's estimated that Paul logged 10,000 miles traveling on these highways. Everything God does has a strategic aspect to it.

In modern times, not only do we have advanced travel, but we have virtual highways to travel around the world with the Good News. In places where it's nearly impossible to openly proclaim the gospel, the message is able to be delivered via internet, shortwave radio and television. Jesus said the following regarding the end-times:

> **Matthew 24:14 And this gospel of the kingdom will be preached in all the world as a witness to all the nations, and then the end will come.**

Tips for Sharing the Gospel

- **Be Kind.** No one has ever yet surrendered to Christ because they were out-argued. We are called to speak the truth in love (Ephesians 4:15). Stop trying to win arguments and focus on winning souls. The Holy Spirit is the convincer, not you (John 16:8).

- **Be Real.** Unbelievers are perceptive and know when someone is "putting on." If you don't know the answer to a question, be honest about it and say you will research it and get back to them. Then get back to the main topic – their salvation.

> No one has ever yet surrendered to Christ because they were out-argued.

- **Be Focused.** When sharing the gospel with someone it may start to feel too personal for them and they might try to shift the conversation to something religious that's less personal. The woman at the well tried this with Jesus. He offered her living water and she wanted to talk about which mountain to worship on (John 4). Gently lead the conversation back to the main topic – their need for Jesus. Their uncomfortability is the conviction of the Holy Spirit.

- **Do Listen.** Jesus always listened when he was saving the lost. Listening to the person's needs and hurts first off shows them you care. It also allows you to be specific with your gospel presentation.

> *Unbeliever*: "I just feel like everyone in my life has let me down."
> *Believer*: "Jesus understands. He created the world, but when He came as a man, the world rejected Him" (John 1:10-11). "Jesus promised that He would never leave us" (Hebrews 13:5).

- **Be Conversational.** Jesus was very conversational when He gained a follower. He talked about things people understood and He related it to spiritual matters and God's truth. He talked about farming, money, building houses, family life and more in order to open their heart to the gospel. Take time to find out about people before you drill them with the Romans Road or the Four Spiritual Laws. Take advantage of the existing conversations you have with friends, neighbors and family to talk about how real Jesus is to you.

> **Make a disciple, not just a convert.**

- **Be Intentional.** By intentional, I mean have a plan to make a disciple, not just a convert. The Great Commission says, *"Go therefore and make disciples of all the nations... teaching them to observe all things that I have commanded you"* (Matthew 28:19-20). If you're unable to personally spend the time needed, try to get them plugged into a good church where they can grow.

- **Be sensitive.** Don't leave the Holy Spirit out of the conversation. You will be much more effective when you allow Him to guide you. The gifts of the Spirit are especially effective in opening people's hearts to the gospel. Consider when Jesus, through the word of knowledge, told the Samaritan woman that she'd had five husbands and the one she was living with now was not her husband (John 4).

> **The gifts of the Spirit are especially effective in opening people's hearts to the gospel.**

- **Be Patient.** Everyone you witness to is not going to immediately accept Jesus as Lord. Be patient and build a relationship if you're able. Allow people to ask questions and express doubt. Work with them as long as they are willing. God's Word never returns void (Isaiah 55:11). In some cases you are sowing seed that someone else will water. But it is God who brings the harvest.

1 Corinthians 3:6 I [Paul] planted, Apollos watered, but God gave the increase.

Being a soul winner is the greatest thing you can do for the kingdom of God. It causes increase in the family of God. The Bible says that God does not want anyone to perish (2 Peter 3:9). But lost people can't be saved unless they hear the gospel and they can't hear the gospel unless someone tells them (Romans 10:14). Put on the gospel shoes of peace and share the Good News!

Chapter Four Review

1. When our focus is _____ in our Christian walk, there is a hole in the armor.

2. What was the early church's source of power for evangelism?

_____

_____

3. What were three keys of evangelism for the early church in the book of Acts?

_____

_____

_____

4. When witnessing, why is it important to be conversational?

_____

_____

_____

_____

Chapter Five: Shield of Faith

Ephesians 6:16 Above all, taking the shield of faith with which you will be able to quench all the fiery darts of the wicked one.

Up until now, every piece of the armor Paul has listed is something to wear. But a shield isn't worn; it's something to *take up*. The Roman soldier's shield was long and rectangular and would cover from knees to chin. It was about three and a half feet long and almost three feet wide.

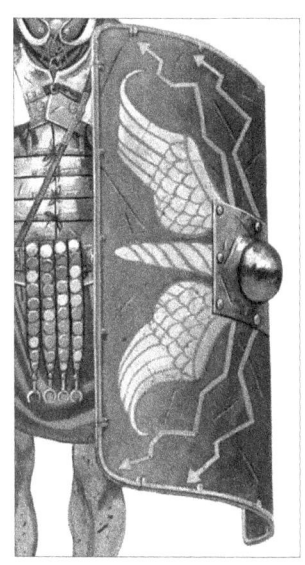

Also, up until now there has been no mention of an incoming attack. Everything has been about getting dressed and being prepared. Now, here in this verse we read about "the fiery darts of the wicked one." At some point, you're going to face a battle. And the only way you're going to overcome is through your faith. Faith is the shield that quenches all the flaming missiles of Satan.

When they had an arrow barrage, they would get on their knees for protection. Similarly, the believer must get on his knees in prayer during times of attack, for faith is utilized through the operation of prayer.

What is Faith?

What exactly is faith? The Bible clearly and definitively answers that question.

> **Hebrews 11:1 Now faith is the substance of things hoped for, the evidence of things not seen.**

Now, let's look at this verse in the Amplified translation:

> **Hebrews 11:1 (AMP) Now faith is the assurance (the confirmation, the title deed) of the things [we] hope for, being the proof of things [we] do not see and the conviction of their reality [faith perceiving as real fact what is not revealed to the senses].**

We hope for things, both in this life and in the one to come. Faith is the vehicle by which we realize those hopes. Faith is the *substance* of things hoped for, or as the Amplified renders it, "the title deed." When you have the title deed to something, it's legally yours even if you haven't seen it yet or put your feet on the ground. God's promises open the door for this kind of faith. Faith perceives as real fact what has not yet been revealed to the senses.

> **Faith perceives as real fact what has not yet been revealed to the senses.**

How Do We Get Faith?

The Bible, once more, is very clear regarding this question.

Romans 10:17 So then faith comes by hearing, and hearing by the word of God.

As can be seen by this verse, faith comes by hearing the word of God – specifically, the *rhema* word of God. This Greek word means, "the spoken word by the living voice." It is when God speaks to you personally out of His Word. Faith comes alive when this happens. But once faith comes, we must do something with it. Many years ago I preached a message on the four stages of faith.

---

1. Faith COMES by Hearing

Romans 10:17 So then faith comes by hearing, and hearing by the word of God.

Faith does not come from *having heard*, but from *hearing*. You must saturate yourself with the Word of God and let it renew your mind.

---

2. Faith is ACTIVATED by Seeing

Hebrews 11:13 These all died in faith, not having received the promises, but having seen them afar off were assured of them, embraced them and confessed that they were strangers and pilgrims on the earth.

At some point, you must begin seeing with the eye of faith what cannot be seen in the natural. See yourself healed... see your husband saved... see yourself being promoted... see your business being successful, etc.

3. Faith is RELEASED by Speaking

2 Corinthians 4:13 And since we have the same spirit of faith, according to what is written, "I believed and therefore I spoke," we also believe and therefore speak.

Ultimately, your faith or your doubt will be located by the words that come out of your mouth. Speak the Word as Jesus taught: *"Whoever says to this mountain, 'Be removed and be cast into the sea,' and does not doubt in his heart, but believes that those things he says will be done, he will have whatever he says"* (Mark 11:23).

4. Faith is CONSUMATED by Doing

James 2:17 Thus also faith by itself, if it does not have works, is dead.

James 2:20 do you want to know, O foolish man, that faith without works is dead?

In the end, our faith must be demonstrated by

> our actions. Like Peter, we must "step out of the boat." Jesus told the lame man, "Take up your bed and walk" (John 5:8). We must act on our faith.

Faith in the Line of Fire

Faith quenches all of the fiery darts of the wicked one. When Satan was attacking Simon Peter, it was Peter's faith that Jesus prayed for.

> **Luke 22:31-32**
> **31 And the Lord said, "Simon, Simon! Indeed, Satan has asked for you, that he may sift you as wheat.**
> **32 But I have prayed for you, that your faith should not fail; and when you have returned to Me, strengthen your brethren."**

Please notice that Satan had to go through Jesus to get to Peter. This is very similar to the story of Job, when Satan petitioned God to give him access to Job's life beyond the hedge. It should be made clear that Jesus knew that Peter would ultimately overcome this test for He told Peter, "When

> **There is no test or trial that we go through that Jesus hasn't already pre-approved us to overcome.**

you have returned to Me," not, "If you return to Me." This is a reality that should stick with each of us. There is no test or trial that we go through that Jesus hasn't already pre-approved us to overcome. This is very much what Paul wrote to the Corinthians.

> **1 Corinthians 10:13 No temptation has overtaken you except such as is common to man; but God is faithful, who will not allow you to be tempted beyond what you are able, but with the temptation will also make the way of escape, that you may be able to bear it.**

The very foundation of our faith is the knowledge that God is *faithful*. I can have faith in a faithful God. Every test that God allows is for the purpose of promoting us, not failing us. After Peter came back from his test, he was promoted. It was Peter who preached the first sermon of the church on the day of Pentecost (Acts 2). It was Peter whom God used to heal the lame man (Acts 3). Three thousand were saved in response to his sermon and five thousand were saved in response to the healing. That's eight thousand who came to know Jesus through the ministry of Peter, right out of the gate. That's incredible promotion.

> **One of the reasons that God allows Satan to continue is to allow our faith to be developed.**

Remember what John wrote: It is the faith of God in our hearts that overcomes the world (I John 5:4). It was Peter's faith that Jesus prayed for. He didn't pray that Peter would be able to avoid the trial, but that his faith would overcome. This is the same prayer that Jesus, your High Priest intercessor is praying for you.

One of the reasons that God allows Satan to continue is to allow our faith to be developed. Faith comes by hearing the Word, but it is exercised when we go through the circumstances of life.

Faith and Bad Circumstances

The Word of Faith movement has long taught that any bad circumstances that persist in your life are a direct result of a lack of faith. Examples of this would be a financial setback or an illness that wasn't healed. The thing is, it *could* be a lack of faith. But that's just one of many variables in situations where suffering is involved.

> We must fight the good fight of faith until all things have been placed under His feet.

To begin with, this whole world is still under the curse of sin – and it will be until Jesus comes back. In this present age, only the soul of a Christian has received the manifestation of redemption. The body, however, is still under the curse of sin. If not, it would never get sick to begin with and it would never die. We wage this battle using the shield of faith in a fallen world. Even though Jesus has already paid the full price for the redemption of all creation, we must fight the good fight of faith until all things have been placed under His feet.

> **Hebrews 2:8 You have put all things in subjection under his feet." For in that He put all in subjection under him, He left nothing that is not put under him. But now we do not yet see all things put under him.**

We see from this verse that all things are *legally* in subjection to Jesus, under His feet. But, *now* in this temporal realm, all things are *not* put under him. This is why faith needs to be a shield. There is opposition!

So, bad things happen to good people – even Christians with faith. It is not safe to assume that problems occur due to a lack of faith any more that it is to assume so due to sin. Either may be a root cause or neither. One thing is for sure – our faith will be tested.

> **Don't be quick to judge someone whose faith is being tested.**

1 Peter 1:7 that the genuineness of your faith, being much more precious than gold that perishes, though it is tested by fire, may be found to praise, honor, and glory at the revelation of Jesus Christ.

Don't be quick to judge someone whose faith is being tested. It's too easy to make assumptions. This is what Job's three friends did when his life got turned upside down. With friends like that, who needs enemies!

Faith That's United

One fascinating aspect about the Roman shield: soldiers could also come together when under attack and hold them over their heads, side by side, and provide a covering – a canopy of protection. Remember, the shield of faith is not only for your personal protection, but also for the body of Christ.

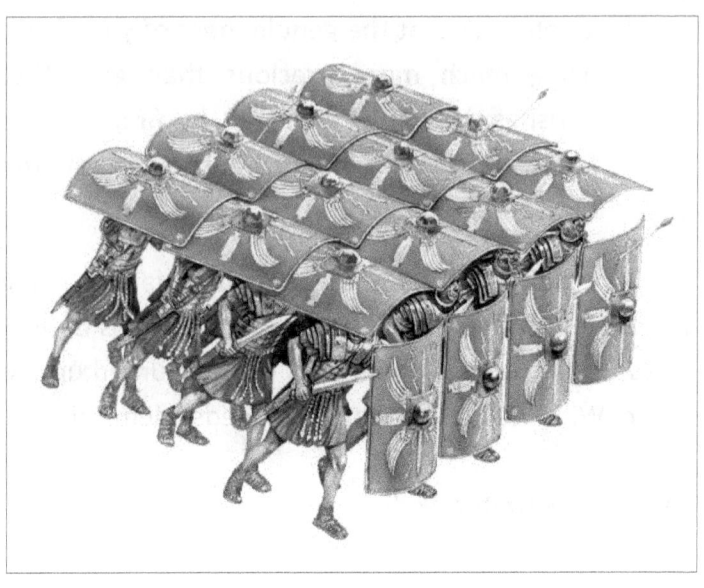

It's always interesting to me how the enemy attacks. Well, maybe *interesting* isn't the right word. When Satan attacks an individual, it is common that he also similarly attacks those in that individual's circle of spiritual connections. I'm not much of a conspiracy theorist, but when it comes to the strategies of Satan, he is always conspiring against the saints of God. For this reason, it is vastly important that you keep in unity with those with whom God has connected you.

> **When Satan attacks an individual, it is common that he also similarly attacks those in that individual's circle of spiritual connections.**

Ordinarily, these will be those you've made friends with at your church.

Jesus taught us to pray in his model prayer (Matthew 6:9-13) to pray in the plural not the singular.

- **Our** Father in heaven (v 9)
- Give **us** this day **our** daily bread (v 11)
- And forgive **us our** debts, as **we** forgive **our** debtors (v 12)
- And do not lead **us** into temptation (v 13)
- But deliver **us** from the evil one (v 13)

Jesus uses nine plural pronouns in this model prayer, teaching us that we should be using our faith to provide a prayer covering for others. United we stand but divided we fall.

Chapter Five Review

1. A shield isn't worn; it's something to _____.

2. What was the purpose of the Roman shield?

_____

_____

3. Fill in the blanks:

> Faith comes by _____
> Faith is activated by _____
> Faith is released by _____
> Faith is consummated by _____

4. What happened with Peter after failing his test?

_____

_____

_____

_____

5. How many plural pronouns did Jesus use in His model prayer?

_____

Chapter Six: Helmet of Salvation

Ephesians 6:17 And take the helmet of salvation...

The Roman soldier's helmet was the best helmet in the ancient world. It provided total protection in the head area. These helmets were primarily made of iron with brass decorations. They weighed slightly more than two pounds. Sometimes there was a crest on top made with horse's hair. This typically signified rank; for instance, centurions would have a crest on their helmets.

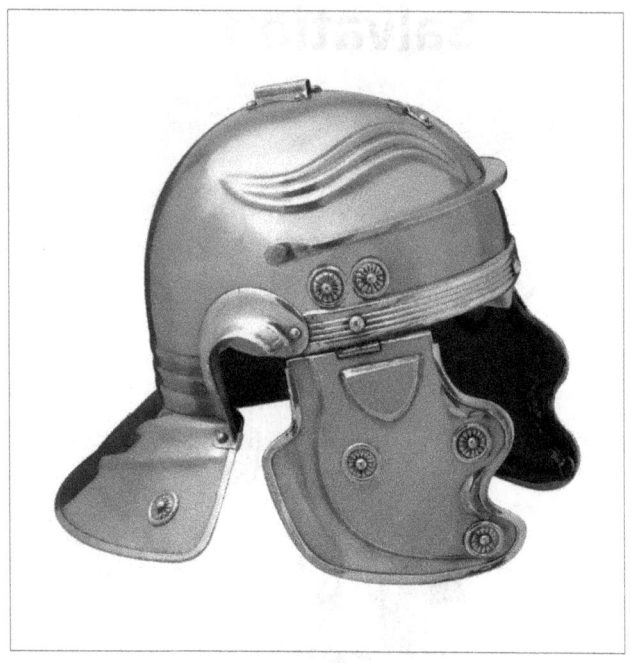

Since the helmet covers the head area, it should be understood that this represents the mind. The importance of protecting the thought life cannot be emphasized enough. Here once again it is reiterated to us that we need to cover our minds with God's armor.

The Mind is the Battlefield

More often than not the mind is the place where Satan finds access through an open door. I always like to tell my church, "The devil is in one of two places in the life of every believer. He can't be both. He is either under your feet or he is between your ears." The devil is a defeated foe so his legal position is beneath your feet (Luke 10:19). But he is also the father of lies (John 8:44) and a master manipulator. He wants to infiltrate the thought life of the believer.

> **The devil is either under your feet or he is between your ears.**

There are two key areas of our thought life that Satan wants to control:

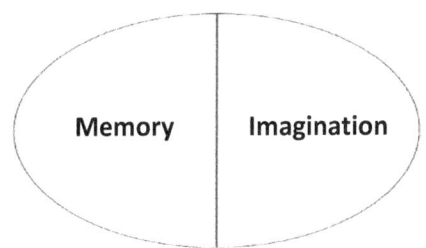

1. The Memory
2. The Imagination

Satan wants to gain access to the memory in order to *replay* the past. Christians are so often hindered by past failures – seemingly never able to overcome the damage done. The devil wants to exploit this and continually remind you of those failures. In this way, it keeps you from moving forward.

For similar reasons, Satan wants access to the imagination in order to *pre-play* the future. Working off the failures of the past, the devil will inject your thoughts of the future with negative outcomes.

Everyone who goes to the movies knows what a trailer is. But why are they called trailers? They are shown before the movie starts, not after. Actually, when the movie industry first started showing them, they were played at the end of the movie, thus the name. But they soon realized people left right after the movie so they moved them to before the movie while you were waiting for the movie to start. But the name trailer stuck. This is kind of how Satan operates. He plays trailers in your mind before you even get started.

> **Satan wants access to the imagination in order to *pre-play* the future.**

We are instructed by the Apostle Paul in the letter to the Philippians to forget the past and reach forward to greater things ahead.

> **Philippians 3:13-15**
> **13** Brethren, I do not count myself to have apprehended; but one thing I do, forgetting

> those things which are behind and reaching forward to those things which are ahead,
>
> **14** I press toward the goal for the prize of the upward call of God in Christ Jesus.
>
> **15** Therefore let us, as many as are mature, have this mind…

You cannot move forward and grow if the past is weighing you down. Paul said, "One thing I do," but then he listed two things: 1) forgetting and 2) reaching. You cannot reach unless you forget and you cannot forget unless you reach. He said this is the *mind* we must have. Too often people forget what they're supposed to remember and remember what they're supposed to forget.

> **Too often people forget what they're supposed to remember and remember what they're supposed to forget.**

Again, all this is played out in the arena of the mind. This is where Satan seeks to gain the advantage. But we are not ignorant of his devices (2 Corinthians 2:11).

Is it the Brain or the Mind?

People often use the terms *brain* and *mind* interchangeably. This is actually incorrect. The brain is part of the body and the mind is part of the soul. I like to explain it this way: if your thinking function were a computer, your brain would be the hardware and your mind would be the software. As we know, having hardware is of not value unless there is software to run the machine.

We renew our mind with the Word of God (Romans 12:2) and it causes the machine of our brain to work the way God intended.

There are two areas of the brain in particular that we will focus on as it relates to the spiritual battle in our mind and renewing the mind.

- **The Limbic System**
- **The Prefrontal Cortex**

The Limbic System is the part of the brain that supplies instinct. Further, it is the emotional center of the brain. Emotions such as anger and pleasure are part of the Limbic System. Long-term memory is stored there. Most interesting, along with the memory, how we *felt* in that moment is stored and recalled as well. So when we are in similar situations, the mind will send out the same feelings as in the original incident. Incredibly, the Limbic System is fully programmed by the age of six.

The Prefrontal Cortex, unlike the Limbic System, is not fully developed until the age of 25. This is the area of the brain that uses judgment, planning, and decision-making. Our moral code is developed in this part of the brain. It is where our emotional *control* resides.

Complex system of nerves and networks in the brain (programmed by age 6) concerned with:	The cerebral cortex that covers the front part of the frontal lobe (not fully developed until age of 25).
<ul><li>Instinct</li><li>Mood</li><li>Emotions</li><li>Fear</li><li>Pleasure</li><li>Anger</li><li>Drives (e.g., hunger, sex)</li><li>Long-term memory</li></ul>	<ul><li>Judgment</li><li>Planning</li><li>Decision-making</li><li>Moral Code</li></ul>

In terms of behavior, the Limbic System is like the *gas pedal* that wants to act on impulse, without regard to good reasoning or moral code. The Prefrontal cortex, on the other hand, is like the *brakes* of the mind. It's not hard to see how this disparity can cause major problems. The adolescent in us wants to act out on impulse. But God's Word tells us that we need to put away childish things.

1 Corinthians 13:11 When I was a child, I spoke as a child, I understood as a child, I thought as a child; but when I became a man, I put away childish things.

The limbic system is constantly on the alert for threats and rewards. Negative or bad things – the threats, get more attention than the positive or good things – the rewards. That's why many people are always emotionally responding in a negative way when bad things happen.

> **The adolescent in us wants to act out on impulse.**

The Limbic System, being wired to react impulsively, holds our long-term memories and the feelings that we had in those moments. When we have gone through a traumatic event as a young person, and later experience something that reminds us of it, the exact same neurons in our brain fire back up and recreate the emotional memory (e.g., rejection). When God heals us of these traumatic events from our past, He doesn't erase our memory of these incidents. Rather, He heals us of the emotional memory and pain that is tied to the traumatic incident. It gives us the ability to remember the occasion without reliving the pain.

The programming in our Limbic System needs to be rewired! It was programmed via nature and nurture. But you don't have to continue to live by that old programming. When you get saved, God gives you a new operating system (sticking with the computer analogy). You have the same hardware, but now you have the Holy Spirit inside you and the Word of God to instruct and renew your mind.

> God gives you a new operating system.

The Thoughts We Choose

Science has finally caught up to the Bible and the truths that were revealed thousands of years ago. The brain is capable of change.

"The thoughts you <u>choose to think</u> are constantly changing your brain's physical structure. Thinking new thoughts causes <u>new neurons to develop</u> and new electrical circuits to be wired to form new patterns of connections. <u>Letting go of old thoughts</u> causes unused neurons to <u>disappear and rewires</u> the electrical circuits within your brain." Dr. Timothy Jennings

Transformation starts by entering a saving relationship with Jesus Christ.

> **2 Corinthians 5:17 Therefore, if anyone is in Christ, he is a new creation; old things have passed away; behold, all things have become new.**

We need to understand the process whereby *old things* pass away and all things *become new*. When you get saved, we get delivered from the *mastery* of sin – but there's still a lot of baggage that we need to be set free from. This is called becoming a *disciple* in the Bible.

> Toxic thinking is one of Satan's greatest tools to defeat believers.

Getting Rid of Toxic Thinking

Toxic thinking is one of Satan's greatest tools to defeat believers. You cannot have on the helmet of salvation and remain in toxicity. As we *consciously* direct our thinking by meditating on the Word of God, we can *wire out* toxic patterns of thinking and replace them with healthy thoughts. When this happens, new *thought networks* grow.

> **Phil. 4:8 Finally, brethren, whatever things are true, whatever things are noble, whatever things are just, whatever things are pure, whatever things are lovely, whatever things are of good report, if there is any virtue and if**

there is anything <u>praiseworthy</u>—MEDITATE [THINK] ON THESE THINGS.

New Pathways

When we choose to think on the promises of God's Word and eliminate the negativity and toxic thinking, something happens in our brain. There are neural pathways in our brain through which information travels. The more we think on something, a path is created, just like a path in the woods is formed by consistently walking the same way. Once the path is created in our brains, it's easy to keep going down the same path.

When we choose to stop thinking negatively and instead fix our minds on the truth of God's Word, those old pathways literally become closed off in our brain. Through consistently thinking on what is true, noble, just, pure, lovely, things of good report and things that are virtuous and praiseworthy, new pathways are formed.

Here is a practical illustration of how applying Philippians 4:8 works.

> **Scenario:** *I've been working really hard on my job and I'm up for a promotion. But as the process started, someone filed a complaint about me that wasn't true.*

I'm very stressed that I might get turned down for the promotion. Someone said I might even lose my job. Instead of worrying, I've decided to put Philippians 4:8 into practice.	
True	Promotion comes from God – Psalm 75:6; 1 Peter 5:6
Noble	Instead of thinking about using what I know about my accuser to get him in trouble, I honorably leave that alone.
Just	I serve a just God who will defend my innocence.
Pure	God knows my heart. Not only didn't I do what was accused of me, but I also have no malice in my heart. I will also wish no evil upon my accuser.
Lovely	I will walk in the love of God and not entertain ill feelings
Good Report	All of my past performance reviews are excellent and I have a good reputation. I choose to think on a positive outcome.
Virtue	I will keep my focus on doing my job with the same excellence I've always done it. Becoming distracted with this would only hurt my performance.
Praiseworthy	I will praise the Lord because He is good to me. He is always faithful and even in the worst case scenario, He

would provide for me.

As we know, different pathways take us to a different destination. We cannot keep doing the same things, thinking the same thoughts, and expect a different result. Another way of saying that is, *what I'm doing right now is the perfect plan to get me the results I'm getting.* If we don't like the results, it's time for a different plan and that starts by changing the way we think.

> **What I'm doing right now is the perfect plan to get me the results I'm getting.**

Once more, we are brought to the importance of renewing our mind.

> **Romans 12:2 And do not be conformed to this world, but be transformed by the renewing of your mind, that you may prove what is that good and acceptable and perfect will of God.**

Remember, this statement was written to Christians, not unbelievers. Transformation is still needed *after* coming to Christ. In some cases, there are *generational curses* that have been in play for three to four generations. Choosing to think God's way will deactivate the generational issues (curses) that have doomed us for so long.

What Does Repentance Mean?

The word *repent*, as used in the New Testament is from the Greek word *metanoeō*, which means, "To change one's mind." Now, what you will find is that preachers will add to the definition and say that it means to change your heart and to change your ways. It's so hard to believe that the word simply means to change your mind. We feel like we're letting people off easy unless we add to the meaning.

> **Repentance means, "To change one's mind."**

Here's the thing, if you really change your mind, your behavior will also change. As for the heart, only God can change the heart. If there is never a change of behavior, there was never really a change of mind. If there is never a change of heart, God knew that the decision to change was insincere. When people try to change their behavior without changing their mind, it is always short-lived.

Moreover, the negative effect of being double-minded cannot be understated. In the letter of James we're told that a double-minded person won't receive anything from the Lord.

> **James 1:6-8**
> **6 But let him ask in faith, with no doubting, for he who doubts is like a wave of the sea driven**

and tossed by the wind.

7 For let not that man suppose that he will receive anything from the Lord;

8 he is a double-minded man, unstable in all his ways.

Double-mindedness is a terrible condition because it keeps you stuck in neutral. It is impossible to be truly repentant while being double-minded. The Greek word for *unstable* (*akatastatos*) literally means "to have anarchy in your mind." This is exactly what Satan wants – your mind to revolt against God's Word. It's time to put on the helmet of salvation!

Tearing Down Strongholds

Paul wrote to the church at Corinth about the subject of the believer being defeated in the arena of the mind. Writing by the Spirit of God, he specifically told them how to gain and maintain the victory.

> **2 Corinthians 10:3-5 (KJV)**
> **3 For though we walk in the flesh, we do not war after the flesh:**
> **4 (For the weapons of our warfare are not carnal, but mighty through God to the pulling down of strongholds;)**
> **5 Casting down imaginations, and every high thing that exalteth itself against the**

knowledge of God, and bringing into captivity every thought to the obedience of Christ

Understanding Mental Strongholds:

By nature, the carnal mind (our selfish orientation) is *hostile* to God. The programming of the natural mind is in opposition to the will of God. It takes the supernatural power of God to tear down strongholds; religion cannot deliver you. Isaiah 10:27 says, "The yoke shall be destroyed because of the anointing."

> **A mental stronghold is a "house made of thoughts."**

A mental stronghold is a "house made of thoughts." Luke 11:24 says that *when an unclean spirit goes out of a man, he seeks rest* (Gr. "an agreeable environment"). Ultimately, the demon wants to return to the "house" he came out of. The enemy does not want to give up the controls he has in your mind.

The stronghold or fortress has three gates:

1. **Eyes:** Job 31:1, "I have made a covenant with my eyes; Why then should I look upon a young woman?" The eyes are a gate that needs paid close attention to. We must make a covenant with our eyes not to indulge in the lust of the

eyes (1 John 2:16).

2. **Ears:** Mark 4:24, "Then He said to them, 'Take heed what you hear.'" Similar to the gate of the eyes, the gate of the ears must be protected. You cannot routinely expose yourself to toxic, negative talk and expect to have a healthy thought life.

3. **Mouth:** Ephesians 4:29, "Let no corrupt word proceed out of your mouth, but what is good for necessary edification, that it may impart grace to the hearers." While some in the word of faith movement have gone to an extreme with confession – name it and claim it, the Bible places extreme importance on the words we speak. If negative and toxic words are coming out of our mouth, it's a sure indicator that the mind has not been renewed.

There are three elements to a stronghold: the outer wall, the inner wall, and the fortress. We will look at them from the inside out:

1. **The Fortress:** the stronghold itself is here. This is where the enemy finds rest – i.e., an agreeable environment. You have thought this way for so long that the stronghold is secure, completely un-dealt with. This mental stronghold is normally held up in the Limbic

System of the mind, where deep-seated emotions and long-term memory are stored.

2. **The Inner Wall:** Imaginations (calculations, reasonings, arguments). Your reasonings must not be sympathetic to your stronghold. Do not allow yourself to justify your attitudes and behavior.

3. **The Outer Wall:** The "high thing" – Pride! The wall is very high and defensive. Pride exalts itself against the knowledge of God. When truth comes, it raises itself ("I already know that," "I don't agree," "so-and-so needs that")

Proverbs 18:11-12 (Amplified): The rich man's wealth is his strong city, and is a high protecting wall in his own imagination and conceit. Haughtiness comes before disaster, but humility before honor.

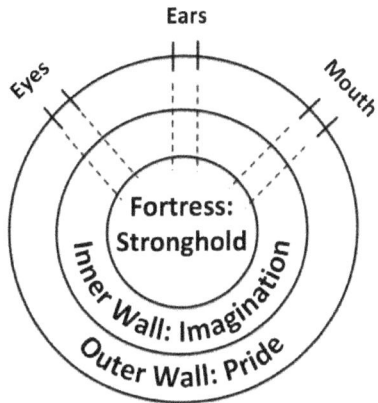

How to Tear Down the Stronghold

This is what you must do in order to tear down the stronghold, the high places of your thought life that are hostile to God.

1. Penetrate the outer wall of pride and admit that you need to be free. This truly is the start point of all help.

    I admit that I need to be free in the following areas:

    _____
    _____
    _____
    _____

2. Stop being sympathetic to the stronghold by making excuses for your attitudes and behavior. There are certainly valid reasons why we behave and think as we do. These are root causes, but should not be used as excuses. If you've been given labels for your condition or disorder, surrender that to God.

   The following reasons are root causes for my strongholds, not excuses:

   _____
   _____
   _____
   _____

3. Finally, by the power of the Holy Spirit and the Word of God, you root out those demonically induced patterns of thinking. Jesus said that, "You shall know the truth and the truth shall make your free" (John 8:32).

   Today, I make a covenant with God to spend time in the Word of God with an intentional focus on the areas of my strongholds.

   Signature:

   _____

   Date:

   _____

Chapter Six Review

1. What are the two areas of a believer's thought life that Satan wants to control?

_____

_____

2. What is the difference between the brain and the mind?

_____

_____

_____

_____

3. The Limbic System is like the _____ of the brain and the Pre-Frontal Cortex is like the _____.

4. What does repentance mean?

_____

_____

5. What are the three parts of a stronghold?

_____

_____

_____

Chapter Seven: Sword of the Spirit (Word of God)

Ephesians 6:17 And take... the sword of the Spirit, which is the word of God.

The Roman sword that Paul was looking at when the Spirit inspired him to pen this description was a *gladius*. It became known as the sword that conquered the world. It was double-edged and relatively short – about 25-27 inches in length. The shortened length made the gladius lethal in close-quarter combat, where longer swords were too cumbersome to be effective.

This is the only offensive weapon in our arsenal. Every other piece of the armor listed has primarily been for defense. The shield could be used to batter but its primary function was to protect. Likewise, the sword could be used to block the enemy's weapon, but its primary function was to thrust and kill the enemy.

> **The sword is the only offensive weapon in our arsenal.**

The Bible

The Bible was written over a 1600-year period by approximately 40 men. The time of the writing was from 1500 BC to AD 95. There are no contradictions in the Bible. Various people claim to have found contradictions, but they have to take verses out of context to do so. When looking at the Bible as a whole and understanding its teachings there are absolutely no contradictions. This is amazing when one considers that the Bible was written over such a long period of time.

There are more than 3,200 verses with fulfilled prophecy either within the Bible itself or since the Bible was written. Amazingly, there are still more than 3,100 verses with unfulfilled prophecies. When it comes to world events and the future, one needs to look no further than the Bible for the answers.

As the Bible itself declares: *"All Scripture is given by inspiration of God, and is profitable for doctrine, for reproof, for correction, for instruction in righteousness"* (2 Timothy 3:16). The early church met at different times in what are known as *Church Councils* to examine the merits of each writing that was being considered for inclusion in the New Testament. It had to have apostolic authorship, or someone closely related to an apostle (e.g., Luke). Further, the writing had to be widely endorsed by the body of Christ at large and be consistent with orthodox doctrine and teaching. Most importantly, the writing had to have clear evidence of being inspired by the Holy Spirit. Just as God inspired or breathed all Scripture, He watched over the formation of the canon of Scripture to ensure the correct books were included. Nothing was left out that should have been included. Moreover, any human error in the translation process has been proven to be miniscule and having no effect on the great doctrines of the Bible.

We can say with complete certainty that we have in our possession the completely inspired, inerrant and infallible Word of the living God.

Satan Cannot Stop God's Word

Many have tried to extinguish the Bible throughout history. The French philosopher Voltaire (1694-1778) predicted in 1776, "One hundred years from my day, there will not be a Bible on earth except one that is looked upon by an antiquarian curiosity-seeker." But within fifty years after his death, the very house in which he once lived was used by the Evangelical Society of Geneva as a storehouse for Bibles and Gospel tracts and the printing presses he used to print his blasphemous publications was used to print Bibles.

Even today, the Bible is illegal in many countries of the world. In some places it's a capital offense to be caught with one. This shows how fearful the devil is of a child of God getting armed with the truth. In spite of the risks, these persecuted believers still do whatever is necessary to get their hands to God's precious Word. In most cases, they will memorize large portions of Scripture because they never know when it will be taken from them.

Over 100 million Bibles are printed every single year. The earth is literally being covered with God's Word!

My Experience

Early in my Christian walk, I fell in love with the Word of God. The very first day I was saved I read all four Gospels. It was all very brand new for me, as I had never read the Bible at all. I also didn't know anyone who was a Christian yet, so there was no one but the Holy Spirit to lead me in my studies. I quickly began to grow in understanding and my hunger for the Word of God increased daily.

It was less than a year after I was saved that I felt the call of God to preach. This only increased my desire to know the Word. Beginning at the age of 21, every day without exception I studied the Bible for no less than five hours a day. Additionally, I prayed for three hours a day. Looking back on it, it sounds kind of legalistic, but it was coming from a true desire to be closer to God and prepare myself to be used by Him. I never missed a day. This continued for about four years. At such time I traveled off to Bible College to receive a formal education in theology. Ultimately, through the years I have continued to pursue formal education and a few years ago earned a Doctor of Ministry in Theology. Through the years I would estimate that I have studied the Bible more than 40,000 hours. The incredible thing is that I still feel like a novice compared to all there is to know.

One of the best things I ever did was to pray through the entire Psalm 119 every night for almost a year. This Psalm portrays David's love and reverence for the Word of God in all 176 verses. It would take me about an hour to personalize it in prayer each night. This occurred about my third year of salvation. Following that time period, God flooded my heart with so much revelation of the Word of God in answer to those prayers. A few years ago I realized a dream, as I was able to write a verse-by-verse devotional commentary on Psalm 119.

Without a doubt, God's Word has been the foundation for my life. It is the light that illuminates my life. It is the lens through which I see the world.

I still have so much to learn and my hunger for God's Word continues to grow.

Symbols of the Word

There are many symbols for the Word of God found in Scripture, in addition to the symbol of the sword.

Food	Matthew 4:4 *But He answered and said, "It is written, 'Man shall not live by bread alone, but by every word that*

	proceeds from the mouth of God.'"
Fire	Jeremiah 20:9 *Then [Jeremiah] said, "I will not make mention of Him, Nor speak anymore in His name." But His word was in my heart like a burning fire Shut up in my bones; I was weary of holding it back, And I could not.*
Hammer	Jeremiah 23:29 *"Is not My word like a fire?" says the LORD, "And like a hammer that breaks the rock in pieces?*
Mirror	James 1:23 *For if anyone is a hearer of the word and not a doer, he is like a man observing his natural face in a mirror.*
Lamp	Psalm 119:105 *Your word is a lamp to my feet And a light to my path.*
Medicine	Proverbs 4:20-22 *My son, attend to my words; incline thine ear unto my sayings. Do not let them depart from your eyes; Keep them in the midst of your heart; For they are life to those who find them, And health to all their flesh.*
Seed	1 Peter 1:23 *Having been born again, not of corruptible seed but incorruptible, through the word of God which lives and abides forever.* Luke 8:11 *"Now the parable is this: The*

	seed is the word of God.

In this study, we will focus on the aspects of the Word of God that relate to the weapon of a sword.

In addition to our primary text in Ephesians 6, the analogy of a sword is also applied to the Word in Hebrews 4.

> **Hebrews 4:12 For the word of God is living and powerful, and sharper than any two-edged sword, piercing even to the division of soul and spirit, and of joints and marrow, and is a discerner of the thoughts and intents of the heart.**

The main point of this passage is that the Word of God is the primary tool of God to be used in self-examination. If we want to reach our full potential in Christ, we must allow His Word to probe all areas including motive and attitude. We cannot afford to use the Word in a superficial way. The Holy Spirit wants to delve deep into the soul and use the Word like a surgical tool to heal. My wife, who is a Doctor of Veterinary Medicine and an excellent surgeon, always likes to say, "A chance to cut is a chance to cure."

> **The Word of God is the primary tool of God to be used in self-examination.**

Before we can ever hope to be effective at using the Word as a weapon against our enemy, we must allow the Word to work in our heart and produce healing and freedom. *Self* is always a much bigger hindrance to serving God than Satan will ever be.

The verse in Hebrews talks about dividing soul and spirit. This simply means separation for clarification. The fastest way I can get someone to understand the difference between soul and spirit is to say that the soul is *self-conscious* and the spirit is *God-conscious*. The table below gives an overview of the primary functions of both soul and spirit.

Self-conscious	*God-conscious*
• Mind	• Intuition
• Will	• Conscience
• Emotion	• Communion

The Word of God is able to discern our innermost thoughts, desires, intentions and motives. This is where John 8:32 comes to pass – the truth makes us free. I always like to say, "The truth will make you free, but first it will make you miserable." The Holy Spirit will use the Word to deal with us in some of the most uncomfortable ways.

So, always allow the Word to point first at you as a surgical tool and then you will be in a position to point it at the enemy as a weapon. And more importantly, to use it as a weapon to defeat the enemy!

> "The truth will make you free, but first it will make you miserable."

Rhema

"Word" in verse 17 is the Greek word *rhema*, meaning "the intimate personal word from God as spoken through His overall Word." Rhema is the same word used in Romans 10:17.

> **Romans 10:17 So then faith comes by hearing, and hearing by the word of God.**

Faith cannot be produced via any other channel. It can only be produced, supernaturally, through hearing and reading the Word, or rhema of God. When you read it you must allow the Holy Spirit to make it personal for you. It must go beyond the words on a page and become God's Word in your heart. There's also a hidden nugget of revelation found in the words of Gabriel to Mary: "For with God nothing will be impossible" (Luke 1:37). The Greek root word translated "nothing" is actually *rhema*. Literally, the verse says, "No rhema from God will be impossible." What a gigantic promise from God!

So when we talk about the sword of the Spirit, it is not *head knowledge* of the Word. An intellectual understanding of the Bible will never defeat the devil. It is the revelation knowledge of the Word spoken out of our mouths from the spirit that will drive back the enemy.

> **An intellectual understanding of the Bible will never defeat the devil.**

Get Behind Me Satan!

This is the weapon that Jesus Himself deployed during His wilderness temptation. Three times Jesus declared "IT IS WRITTEN!" until Satan had to flee! Of course, Satan was trying to provoke Jesus to prove his deity in some random way like turning stones into bread. This would have taken Jesus out of His mission to live a perfect sinless life as a man and redeem lost humanity. Jesus, instead, exercised great self-control and used the authority of the Word of God to defeat Satan.

The verses below were the third and final encounter (for that season):

Matthew 4:10-11

**10 Then Jesus said to him, "Away with you, Satan! For it is written, 'You shall worship the Lord your God, and Him only you shall serve.'"
11 Then the devil left Him...**

Please note that if Jesus has to keep reinforcing His position with the Word then you and I will need to do the same. It's not about just saying it once or twice. But keep thrusting the gladius of the Word into the heart of Satan. God's Word never returns void (Isaiah 55:11).

We can also take away from this encounter that Jesus had with Satan that God's voice is not the only one heard in the wilderness, while under temptation. When under duress, Satan will try to counterfeit the voice of God to get you to act compulsively – out of the will of God. With Jesus, the enemy quoted Psalm 91 but used it out of context. But Jesus knew the Word and responded that He was not to tempt the Lord His God. One thing that was central to all the temptations is Satan's push to get Jesus to validate Himself. But Jesus didn't take the bait. He had just been baptized and been affirmed by His Father.

**Matthew 3:16-17
16 When He had been baptized, Jesus came up immediately from the water; and behold, the heavens were opened to Him, and He saw the**

Spirit of God descending like a dove and alighting upon Him.

17 And suddenly a voice came from heaven, saying, "This is My beloved Son, in whom I am well pleased."

The Word will validate and affirm you in the Father's love and complete acceptance. Don't live your life trying to prove something based on a lack of earthly validation. This is the trap of Satan.

Revelation Knowledge

Satan knows the written Word. He tried to use it against Jesus by twisting the meaning of Psalm 91:11-12 and taking it out of context. He could quote the entire Bible from cover to cover, but he has no revelation knowledge of the Truth because he is cut off from

> Satan has no revelation knowledge of the Truth

the life of God. Ephesians 4:18 says that when one is alienated from the life of God, their understanding is darkened and they are spiritually blind. This is the condition of Satan, a fallen angel. Revelation knowledge of the Word of God is a weapon for which he has no defense!

Roman soldiers were taught to thrust with their gladius sword, not slash. A stroke with the edge rarely kills, but a stab is usually fatal. The *rhema* of God is like a pinpoint stab into Satan's unprotected area.

Applying the Truth of God's Word

It's one thing to say that we believe God's Word, but quite another to put it into practice. James wrote, "Tell me all you want about your faith, but I'll show you mine by what I do" (paraphrased). It is the application of God's Word that serves as a sword of the Spirit and drives the enemy back. Of course, this must be preceded by a faith in the heart and a renewing of the mind. But when you align those three forces, you become unstoppable.

How to be Unstoppable:

1. Have faith in your heart
2. Renew your mind
3. Put God's Word into practice

Developing godly habits based on Scripture is the clear path to living the overcomer's life. It's what we do in the small areas of life that add up to the big victories. Putting God's Word into practice keeps the believer on the offense and driving Satan backwards.

Chapter Seven Review

1. What is the advantage of a shorter gladius sword over a longer traditional sword?

_____

_____

_____

_____

2. List at least three other symbols of the Word of God?

_____

_____

_____

3. What is the main application of the Word, as described in Hebrews 4:12?

_____

_____

_____

_____

4. What is a rhema word of God?

_____

_____

_____

Chapter Eight: Prayer

Ephesians 6:18-19
18 praying always with all prayer and supplication in the Spirit, being watchful to this end with all perseverance and supplication for all the saints—
19 and for me, that utterance may be given to me, that I may open my mouth boldly to make known the mystery of the gospel.

Prayer, as presented here, is not a weapon per say, but the place in which the weapons are put to use. The armor is not just a metaphor without any practical value. The armor is dynamic in its working when utilized in prayer. This is the battleground, where the battle is fought and won. Satan trembles when the weakest saint of God gets on his knees to pray. Satan is not fearful of men of *standing*, but rather men of *kneeling*.

Spiritual warfare is conducted first in the prayer closet. Daniel chapter 10 reveals the nature of this warfare and the Believer's role in standing for the breakthrough.

> **Daniel 10:12-14**
> **12 Then he said to me, "Do not fear, Daniel, for from the first day that you set your heart to understand, and to humble yourself before your God, your words were heard; and I have come because of your words.**
> **13 But the prince of the kingdom of Persia withstood me twenty-one days; and behold, Michael, one of the chief princes, came to help me, for I had been left alone there with the kings of Persia.**
> **14 Now I have come to make you understand what will happen to your people in the latter days, for the vision refers to many days yet to come."**

There are several key takeaways from this passage:

- The angel Gabriel told Daniel that God heard his prayer from the very first day he began to seek God. This is so important to remember when we get weary. God is moving, but we often fail to see it in the natural. It can feel as if God isn't listening. But this is a lie from Satan to discourage us to quit.

- There was warfare in the heavenlies as a result of God sending Gabriel with the answer. Gabriel was the Archangel of Communication and though he was powerful, warfare was not his specialty. Consequently, he enlisted the aid of his counterpart, Michael – the Archangel of Warfare.

- Gabriel, with the assistance of Michael, broke through the resistance of the dark prince of Persia. This was either Satan himself or one of his top principalities. There will always be resistance when we pray – especially if we are praying about kingdom matters.

- Even though Daniel was weakened from the 21-day fast, he persevered anyway. The breakthrough happened at a time when he likely felt like giving up. It's so important not to quit when you feel discouraged. God will never allow you to be tempted beyond your spiritual ability to overcome (1 Corinthians 10:13).

Different Kinds of Prayer

There are different kinds of prayer listed by Paul in Ephesians chapter six:

Prayer in the Spirit:

There are levels of prayer that can only be accomplished in the Spirit. Praying in other tongues in intercession opens up a whole new arena of power in our lives, for Satan has no power over our heavenly language. While some reading may disagree that tongues are for today, I'd challenge that position with the Word of God. There is positively no verse in the New Testament that says tongues will be done away with other than when the perfect kingdom comes (1 Corinthians 13). Paul wrote, "Do not forbid to speak with tongues" (1 Corinthians 14:39). I have written a book on prophecy and tongues and in that book I refute every argument against speaking in tongues and also show the proper order for tongues in the church.

> **There is positively no verse in the New Testament that says tongues will be done away with other than when the perfect kingdom comes.**

On a personal note, I must say that the gift of tongues in my prayer life has had the second greatest impact on my spiritual development, second only to the Bible. Not a day goes by that I don't pray in the Spirit. When a Christian prays in the Spirit, the perfect will of God is being prayed for (Romans 8:27).

Supplication:

This refers to making specific requests to God. If you are looking for a generic answer then make a generic prayer. If you need something specific then first make sure it lines up with the Word of God and then pray specifically. It's amazing how many prayers that people can pray that lack any specificity. Jesus said, "Whatever things you ask when you pray, believe that you receive them, and you will have them" (Mark 11:24). This is referring to *specific things* that you desire.

Keeping a prayer journal is helpful in tracking specific prayer requests. I began doing this some time back and it has greatly enhanced my prayer life. It keeps me focused, plus it allows me to look back and see answered prayer that I may have otherwise forgotten.

If possible, extend prayer to others: "Give **us** this day **our** daily bread" (Matt. 6:11).

Watchful Prayer:

This is intercessory prayer. Essentially, it is taking up God's cause and going through the birthing process until the Holy Spirit releases you – or when you have "given birth" in the Spirit.

Examples of Intercessory Prayer in the Bible:

- Abraham for Sodom (Genesis 18:20-23)
- Moses for Israel (Exodus 32:31-32)
- Ezra – cleansing for Gods people (Ezra 9:6-15)

- Paul's for the Ephesians (Ephesians 3:14-20)
- Paul's for the Colossians (Colossians 1:9-12)

Another example is in Acts chapter 12 when the church prayed persistently for Peter to be delivered and God sent an angel to deliver him from prison. Some have a greater calling and gifting in this area than others. But all should use this type of prayer.

Persevering Prayer:

There are times when the believer must ask, seek and knock in order to get the answer (Matthew 7:7). Jesus also called this persistent prayer – a refusal to be denied

> **Luke 11:5-8**
> **5 And He said to them, "Which of you shall have a friend, and go to him at midnight and say to him, 'Friend, lend me three loaves;**
> **6 for a friend of mine has come to me on his journey, and I have nothing to set before him';**
> **7 and he will answer from within and say, 'Do not trouble me; the door is now shut, and my children are with me in bed; I cannot rise and give to you'?**
> **8 I say to you, though he will not rise and give to him because he is his friend, yet because of his persistence he will rise and give him as many as he needs.**

9 So I say to you, ask, and it will be given to you; seek, and you will find; knock, and it will be opened to you."

It is not as though God is indifferent, as the neighbor in the parable seems to be. It's just that during times when prayer is waiting to be answered, it can *feel* that way. The point Jesus is making is the need for persistence. Often during times of persistent prayer, God will peel back the layers of selfish motivation in the process. Rest assured, God is always on time!

Prayer for God's Leaders:
In verse 19 Paul clearly expressed the need for the saints to pray for him that God would give him utterance and that he would speak boldly. Much of what is coming forth from the pulpit is based on the prayer of the church (or lack thereof). If the church wants a prophetic word from God, then much prayer is required.

Personally, there are times when I feel weakened or discouraged in the ministry. But at just the right time, God will put me on someone's heart to pray. Through their intercession I feel strength and courage enter my soul. It's hard to explain how I know that it's due to the prayers of the saints, but I just know.

Always remember to pray for your pastor and your spiritual leaders. Below are some of the things you can pray for them about:

- God's protection – both physical and spiritual
- Family – blessing, guidance, unity and protection
- Knowledge – fill the pastor with revelation knowledge
- Purity – live a life of sanctification and holiness
- Focus – stay true to the assignment given by God
- Care for the flock – wisdom, discernment and compassion

Additionally, the Bible mentions other types of prayer:

Prayer of Faith:
This is prayer that is in agreement with God's Word and its promises. When you pray in accordance with God's Word, it is never a matter of "If it be Thy will." If the Word explicitly reveals His will on a particular matter, you may exercise the prayer of faith with certainty. The New Testament is filled with promises regarding this type of prayer.

> **Mark 11:24 Therefore I say to you, whatever things you ask when you pray, believe that you receive them, and you will have them.**

James 5:15 And the prayer of faith will save the sick, and the Lord will raise him up...

Prayer of Blessing:
The prayer of blessing happens when the anointing of the Holy Spirit is upon the person praying. This prayer is most often utilized with the laying on of hands. It is an impartation of God's grace and virtue. God is using the person praying as a conduit to flow through into the other person's spiritual and/or physical life.

When God is using someone in this fashion, it is always best to take advantage of the moment. As an example, every Sunday in my church there is an altar call for people to come forward for prayer and ministry. It is common for the Holy Spirit to move in such a way that people are saved, healed and delivered. There is a special anointing because God is confirming the Word that was preached and people are responding in faith. However, I've had numerous instances when people waited and instead of coming forward, they waited until after the service was over and requested prayer in my office, in the foyer or on the parking lot. I'm always happy to pray for anyone in need, but at that point, it becomes a prayer of faith and not a prayer of blessing. The anointing is not something that can be turned off and on.

Prayer of Agreement:

> **Matthew 18:18-20**
> **18 "Assuredly, I say to you, whatever you bind on earth will be bound in heaven, and whatever you loose on earth will be loosed in heaven.**
> **19 "Again I say to you that if two of you agree on earth concerning anything that they ask, it will be done for them by My Father in heaven.**
> **20 For where two or three are gathered together in My name, I am there in the midst of them."**

This type of prayer is when you join together with one ore more other believers to agree in prayer on a specific request. The agreement extends beyond the request and also relates to overall unity and accord. What I mean by this is

> **You can't be in discord with your brother, but simply agree in prayer.**

you can't be in discord with your brother, but simply agree in prayer. There must be a unity that precedes the prayer.

There is an old promise in the book of Deuteronomy that says, *"One can chase a thousand and two can put ten thousand to flight"* (Deuteronomy 32:30). God is saying that two working in agreement will multiply the result by ten! This is why Satan fights unity in the church so fiercely. He knows the power that comes from agreement.

Prayer of Praise & Worship:
This is the form of prayer that does not ask for anything. It is seeking the Lord's *face* (His presence), not His *hand* (His acts).

> **Hebrews 13:15 Therefore by Him let us continually offer the sacrifice of praise to God, that is, the fruit of our lips, giving thanks to His name.**

It is important to spend time each day giving praise and worship to God. He is worthy of our praise. It should be noted that the Lord's model prayer (Matthew 6:9-13) both begins and ends with worship.

> **This is the form of prayer that does not ask for anything.**

> Start (v 9): *"Our Father in heaven, hallowed be Your name."*
>
> Finish (v 13): *"For Yours is the kingdom and the power and the glory forever. Amen."*

The book of Psalms is a great resource for inspiration. It is filled with real worship from real people in times of real struggle. It is incredible how David or one of the other psalmists hit rock bottom, emotionally. But through the act of remembering the goodness of God, would begin to praise and worship Him. We must live a life of continual thankfulness to God.

Prayer of Consecration:
> **Matthew 6:10 Your kingdom come. Your will be done on earth as it is in heaven.**

This type of prayer, the prayer of consecration, is how one discovers the unique and individual components of God's will for his or her life. There are many occasions in life when it is appropriate to pray, "If it be Thy will." In the passage below, we see the example of Jesus in the garden of Gethsemane, praying for the Father's will. The very name Gethsemane means, "oil press." It was a place designed for pressure and in this instance the Son of God was experiencing the weight of the world as He came to terms with His fate on Calvary.

Luke 22:41-42

41 And He was withdrawn from them about a stone's throw, and He knelt down and prayed, 42 saying, "Father, if it is Your will, take this cup away from Me; nevertheless not My will, but Yours, be done."

Throughout my life and ministry there have been many times when I wrestled with the will of God, seeking to understand what God was doing in my life. In most cases I was able to work through things and obediently continue in God's will with the right decisions. But there have been a handful of times when I missed God for various reasons – none good. In one such case, I had an opportunity to leave the church I was pastoring in Indiana and take a new church in North Carolina. In the natural, everything was lining up. Doors were opening and my house sold quickly. But deep down I was troubled in my spirit. There was a definite absence of peace. But I chose to ignore it. I'd made up my mind. To make a long story short, it was disastrous. It took nearly two years to recover from that bad decision and it was all because I wouldn't listen to the Holy Spirit when He tried to warn me.

In the prayer of consecration, don't pray for God's will if you aren't willing to accept what you might not like. God is the only one who knows the future. When He warns you, it's for good reason.

The power of a prayer life is the greatest force in life. The spiritual battle we are in is real and without the armor of God and prayer, we are severely limited and at a disadvantage.

"Put on the whole armor of God, that you may be able to stand against the wiles of the devil." (Ephesians 6:11)

Chapter Eight Review

1. When did God hear Daniel's prayer?

_____

_____

2. Who was the prince of Persia?

_____

_____

3. When will the gift of tongues be done away with?

_____

_____

_____

_____

4. What is another name for watchful prayer?

_____

5. What is the difference between the prayer of faith and the prayer of consecration?

_____

_____

_____

_____

Other Books by David Chapman

All books may be purchased through Amazon

Thy Word: A Devotional Commentary on Psalm 119 Apr 17, 2019
by David A. Chapman
Paperback
$10⁰⁰ ✓prime

Other Formats: Kindle Edition

The Power of Praise: The 7 Hebrew Words for Praise May 27, 2014
by David Chapman
Paperback
$10⁰⁰ ✓prime

Other Formats: Kindle Edition

The Believer's Deliverance Handbook: 7 Levels of Demonic Involvement and How to Minister Deliverance
Jan 29, 2014
by David Chapman
Paperback
$7⁰⁰ ✓prime

Other Formats: Kindle Edition

Caught Up: The Rapture of the Church Jun 24, 2015
by David Chapman
Paperback
$10⁰⁰ √prime

Other Formats: Kindle Edition

Modern Day Apostles: The Supernatural Ministry of the Apostle in the Modern Day Church Mar 4, 2014
by David Chapman
Paperback
$10⁰⁰ √prime

Other Formats: Kindle Edition

The Kingdom Within Aug 17, 2016
by David Chapman
Paperback
$9⁷⁸ $12.00 √prime

Other Formats: Kindle Edition

Knowing God's Will: & Walking in His Blessing Nov 15, 2014
by David Chapman
Paperback
$10⁰⁰ √prime

Other Formats: Kindle Edition , Mass Market Paperback

The Power of the Anointing Dec 7, 2014
by David Chapman
Paperback
$10⁰⁰ ✓prime

Other Formats: Kindle Edition

Overcoming Life's Enemies Sep 10, 2016
by David Chapman
Paperback
$10⁰⁰ ✓prime

Other Formats: Kindle Edition

Unlocking the Power of Honor Aug 9, 2018
by David Chapman
Paperback
$10⁰⁰ ✓prime

Counted Faithful: Verse-by-Verse Commentary on I Timothy Jun 1, 2017
by Dr. David Chapman
Paperback
$12⁰⁰ ✓prime

Other Formats: Kindle Edition

The Pattern & The Glory: The New Testament Pattern for the Glorious End-Time Church Jul 30, 2015
by David Chapman
Paperback
$12⁰⁰ prime

Other Formats: Kindle Edition

Thus Saith The Lord: Prophecy & Tongues May 15, 2014
by David Chapman
Paperback
$8⁰⁰ prime

Other Formats: Kindle Edition

The Seven Letters of Jesus: God's Message to the End-Time Church Nov 16, 2015
by David A Chapman
Paperback
$10⁰⁰ prime

Other Formats: Kindle Edition

The Fullness of the Spirit: How to be Filled with the Holy Spirit & Walk in Victory Feb 26, 2014
by David A Chapman
Paperback
$10⁰⁰ prime

Other Formats: Kindle Edition

Blood Covenant: The Power of the Blood of Jesus Feb 3, 2014
by David Chapman
Paperback
$10⁰⁰ ✓prime

Other Formats: Kindle Edition

The Fruitful Life Mar 3, 2020
by David Chapman
Paperback
$10.00
Usually ships within 3 days.
More Buying Choices
$10.00 (6 Used & New offers)

Building Altars: Becoming a Living Sacrifice Jun 11, 2020
by David Chapman
$4.99
In this book we will examine each example in the Bible where an altar was built. We will look at the reason it was built as well as the spiritual application. Some of the topics covered include:•The purpose of altars in

⌄ Read more

Other Formats: Paperback

You may contact David Chapman by writing to:

TRU Publishing
Attn: David Chapman
1726 S. 1st Ave.
Safford, Arizona 85546

Or by emailing:
TheRiverAZ@gmail.com

www.ingramcontent.com/pod-product-compliance
Lightning Source LLC
Chambersburg PA
CBHW060329050426
42449CB00011B/2707